Believe

written and Illustrated by
pattie welek hall

To contact Pattie or to order copies of this book please visit her website at:
www.pattiewelekhall.com

A portion of the sales of this book will be donated to the
Casa de Santa Maria, in San Luis, Colorado,
whose mission is to heal broken hearts, offer clarity of purpose
and bring comfort, peace and joy to the soul.
www.casadesantamaria.org

ISBN: 1449990002
EAN-13 is 9781449990008

From: _____

To: _____

Dedication

This book is dedicated to
Robert Burns Hall Jr. (Bo),
The Hall family,
and all families who walked
in these same shoes.

Believe

"Why did you let all the balloons go,
Oma? Do you like to watch them dance
in the sky?"

"What's wrong, Oma?
Why are you crying?"

"So many questions for a little one."

"Tell me... tell me... Please, Oma!"

"Come. Sit on my lap, little one. Long
ago, I had a son who looked just like you.
He went to heaven at a very early age.
Today is his birthday."

"How old was he when he went to heaven, Oma? Was he five like me?"

Oma laughs. "No, little one, he was 22."

"Ohhh... that's old!"

"To you it is. To me, his mama, 22 was quite young."

"Why did he go to heaven so soon?
Didn't he like it here?"

"Now that's a hard question even for your Oma. Sometimes we just have to trust that life is exactly the way it is OR... it would be different."

"Were you sad, Oma?"

"Oh... very sad, my love."

19

"Did you cry Oma?"

"Yes... yes, I did. Some days I still cry.
It's hard to lose the ones we love."

"Remember last spring when you decided you were tired of your cockatiel being stuck in his cage? You said you wanted Bubba to be "free" so he could spread his wings and fly like all the other birdies. Remember?"

23

"I do! I opened Bubba's cage and he went 'fffttt' right out the window. I was so sad. I cried a lot. I loved Bubba and I wanted him to come back."

"I miss Bubba, Oma, a whole... whole bunch! I can't hold him anymore and talk to him...

listen to him sing funny music...

watch him make a mess when he plays...

31

see how big he gets...

and give him kisses all over."

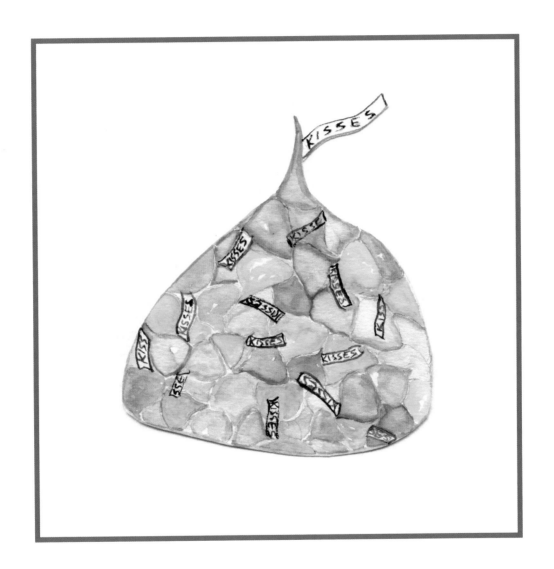

"I understand, my prescious. That's how Oma feels about losing her son. There will always be a hole in my heart. All the things you miss about Bubba, I miss about my son... holding him... having conversations with him... listening to his voice... his laughter... his crazy music... watching him play and grow... giving him bunches of hugs, kisses and all my love."

"Does the sadness ever go away, Oma?"

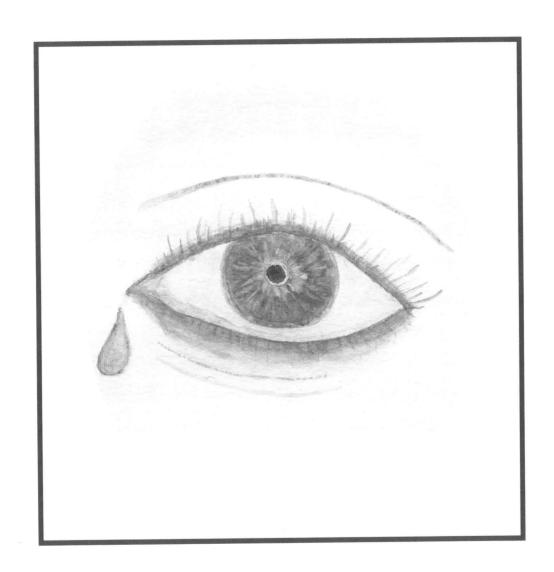

"I don't know about that, my love. What I do know is you can change how you think. By focusing on the good times... the laughter... the love... the uniqueness of the child's soul... the lessons your child came to teach... and the gifts your child left behind... you can find peace in your heart."

"Do all people leave behind gifts when they go to heaven, Oma?"

"I believe they do. Sometimes it takes some extra digging to find them, but they are there."

"Can you send gifts to heaven, Oma?"

"Yes, you can! I fill each balloon with a special gift from my heart."

"You do?"

"Yes."

"That's like magic!"

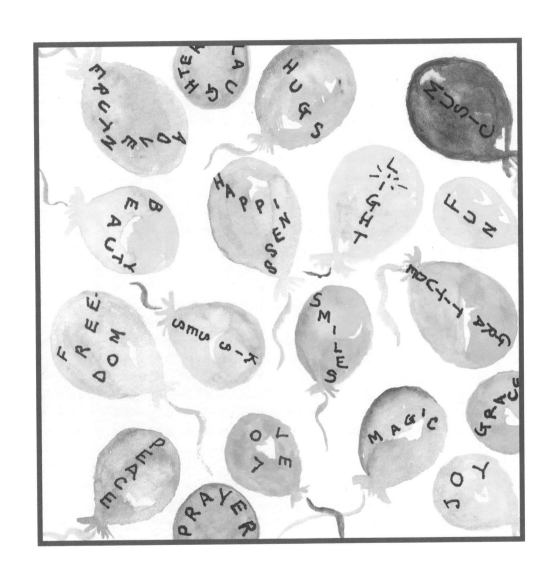

"The balloons are a celebration of my son's life... his beauty... his grace. Even though he isn't physically here, I want him to know how "special" he is... that his spirit is alive in my heart... and that I will always honor his journey on earth."

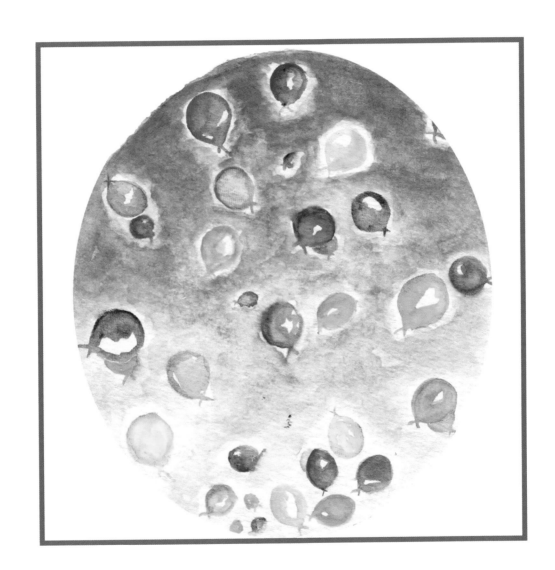

"Besides that I want to make sure the angels don't forget the balloons for his party tonight in heaven!"

"How do you know he will get them, Oma? It's a long... long... long way up to heaven."

"Sometimes, my love, you just have to BELIEVE!"

"Got 'em!

Thanks... thanks... thanks...
Mom... Mom... Mom...

Love... love... love...
You... you... you!"

Though the voice is quiet,
the spirit still echoes.

Made in the USA
Charleston, SC
19 January 2010